PATHS
The Journey Awaits

By GW Tolley

GW Tolley is an International Author, Self-Publishing Coach, Udemy Instructor (SELF PUBLISHING-Outside the Box), Amazon Best Sellers Rank, Writer / Executive Producer of "i am JOSIAH" Project, TV Host / Executive Producer of "What's Your Story," Co-Host of Lessons For Life/Abundant TV, Google Influencer (76+ Million views), Podcaster, YouTuber, Awareness Advocate (Homeless, Underprivileged, Hearing Impaired and Deaf), WRITE It OUT Program (Firefighters, First Responders, Military, and Police Officers) = all this is God's doing.

Special Thank you to my dad.

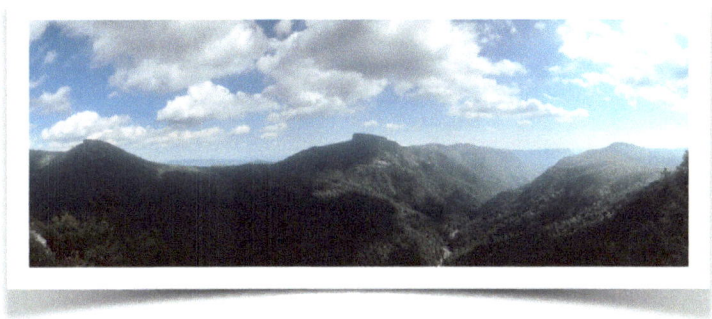

Paths, the unseen, the road less traveled. Life has many paths, some leading to the mountain's peak, others deep into the valley. The seasons play their part, altering landscapes, altering us. Each of Winter's frost, spring's bloom, summer's blaze, or autumn's fall has a lesson to teach. Each path, right or wrong, shapes us and molds us.

We might travel with companions, sharing laughter and tears, or travel solo. But are we ever truly alone? Remember, weary traveler, to pause, to breathe. Rest under a tree, stop and smell the flowers, or relax by the babbling brook. The paths can be difficult sometimes, but enjoy the ride, cherish the moments, and most importantly, enjoy the journey.

Table of Content

The Journey Begins

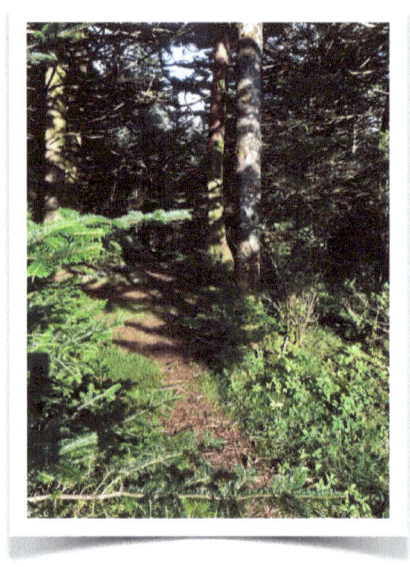

Trust in the Lord with all your heart and lean not on your own understanding; in all your ways submit to him, and he will make your paths straight.
Proverbs 3:5-6 NIV

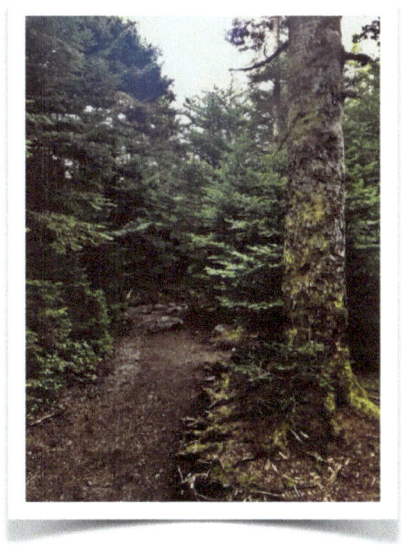

A person's steps are directed by the Lord. How then can anyone understand their own way?
Proverbs 20:24 NIV

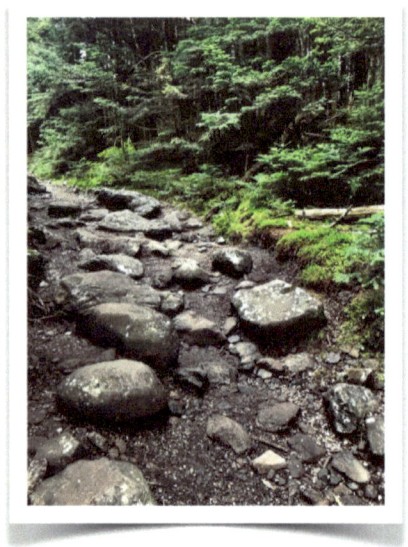

"A stone that causes people to stumble and a rock that makes them fall." They stumble because they disobey the message which is also what they were destined for. 1 Peter 2:8 NIV

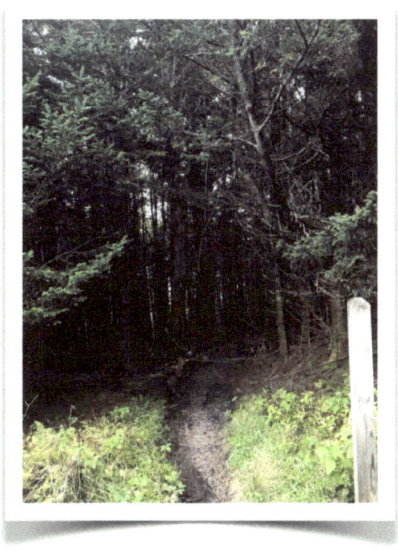

Give careful thought to the paths for your feet and
be steadfast in all your ways. Proverbs 4:26 NIV

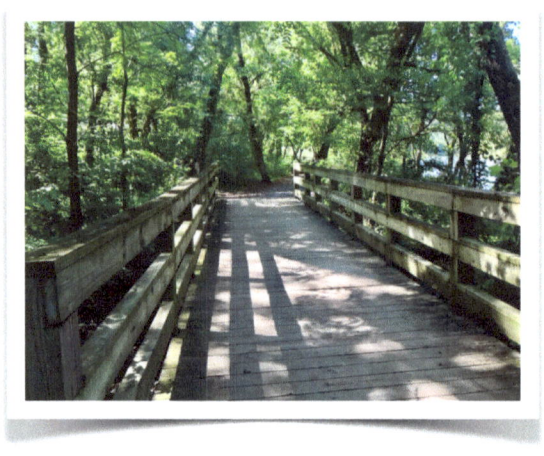

He refreshes my soul.
He guides me along the right
paths for his name's sake. Psalm 23:3 NIV

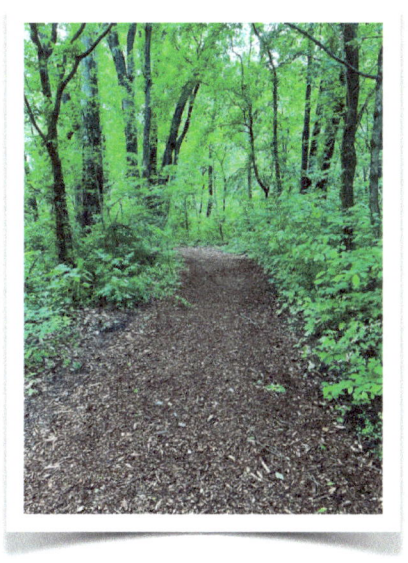

Your word is a lamp for my feet,
a light on my path. Psalm 119:105 NIV

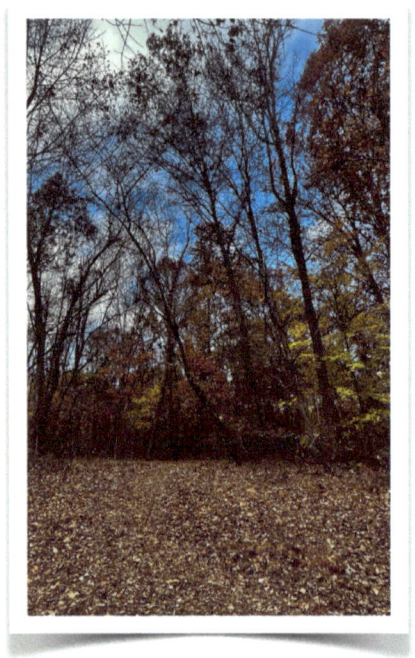

Whether you turn to the right or to the left,
your ears will hear a voice behind you, saying,
"This is the way; walk in it." Isaiah 30:21 NIV

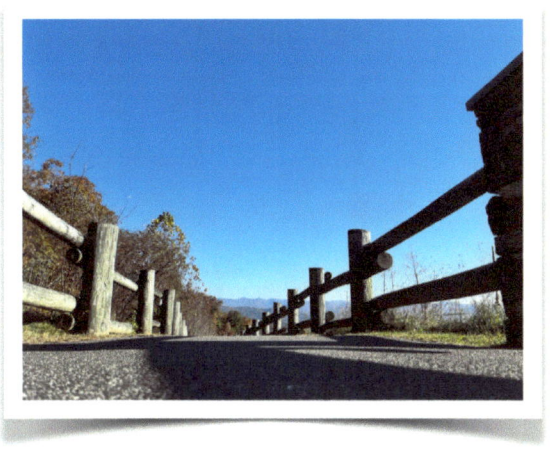

In their hearts humans plan their course,
but the Lord establishes their steps.
Proverbs 16:9 NIV

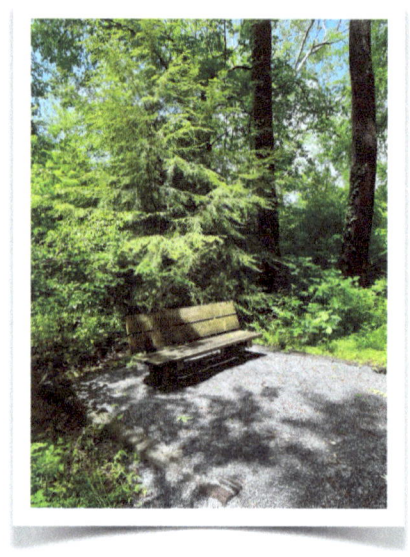

Yes, my soul, find rest in God;
my hope comes from him.
Psalm 62:5 NIV

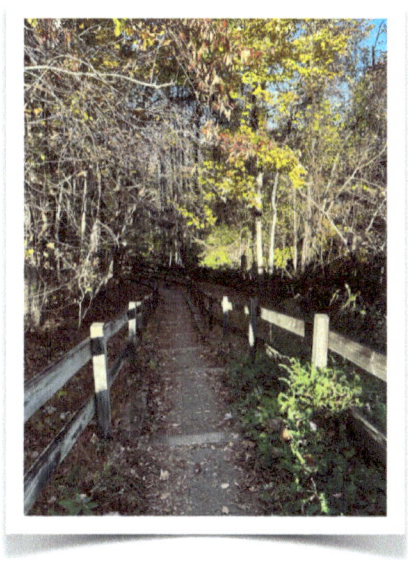

You make known to me the path of life; you
will fill me with joy in your presence, with
eternal pleasures at your right hand.
Psalm 16:11 NIV

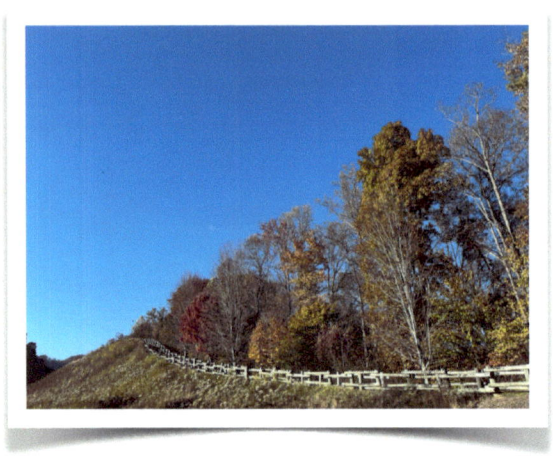

When Jesus spoke again to the people, he said, "I am the light of the world. Whoever follows me will never walk in darkness, but will have the light of life." John 8:12 NIV

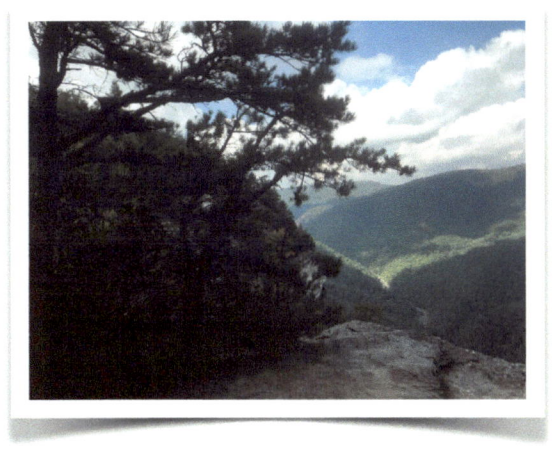

He guides the humble in what is right
and teaches them his way.
Psalm 25:9 NIV

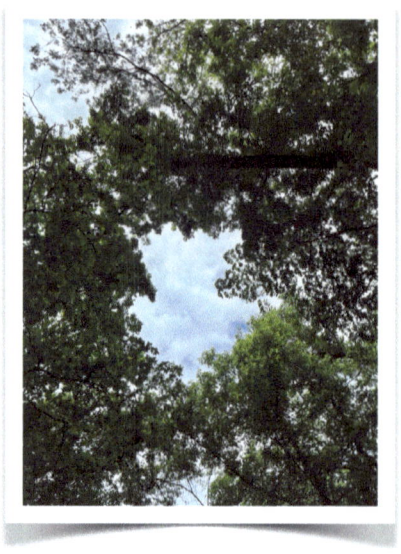

I will instruct you and teach you in the way
you should go; I will counsel you with my
loving eye on you. Psalm 32:8 NIV

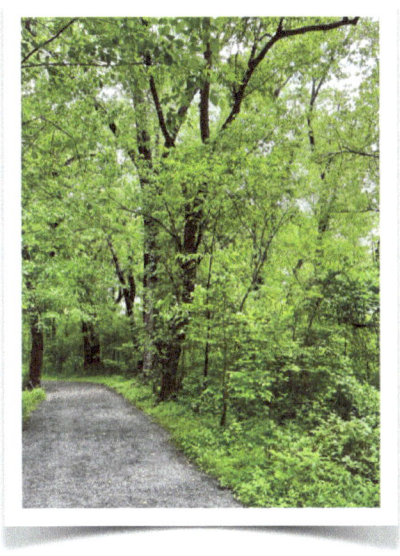

This is what the Lord says—your Redeemer, the Holy One of Israel: "I am the Lord your God, who teaches you what is best for you, who directs you in the way you should go. Isaiah 48:17 NIV

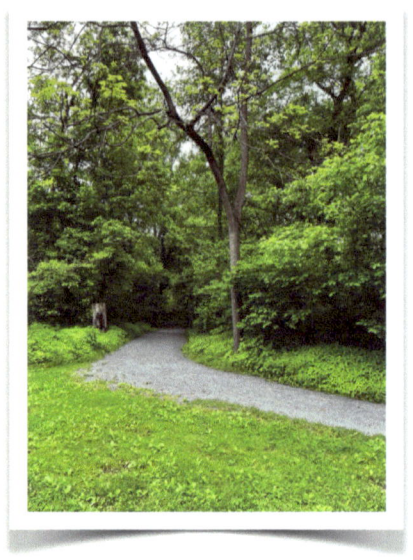

The Lord makes firm the steps
of the one who delights in him
Psalm 37:23 NIV

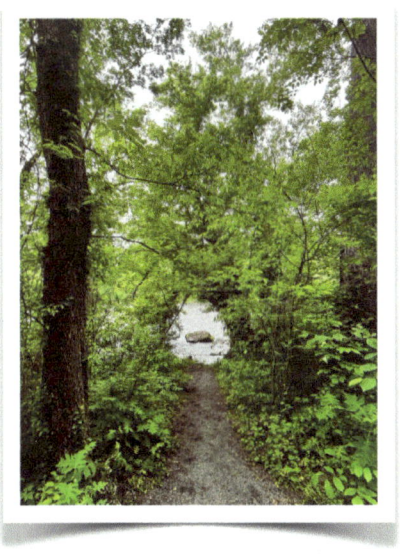

The Lord will guide you always; he will satisfy your needs in a sun-scorched land and will strengthen your frame. You will be like a well-watered garden, like a spring whose waters never fail. Isaiah 58:11NIV

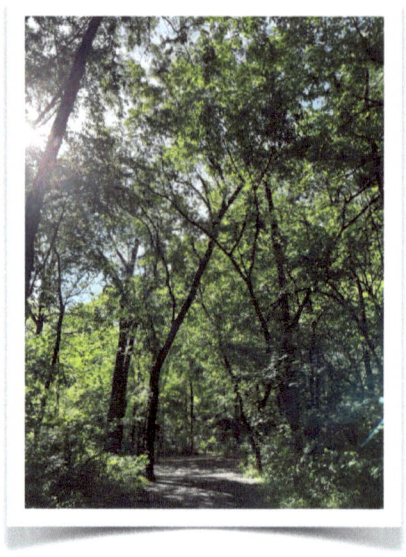

Train up a child in the way he
should go; even when he is old
he will not depart from it.
Proverbs 22:6 NIV

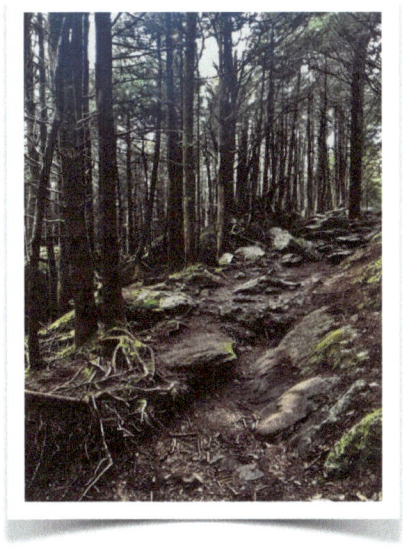

My sheep listen to my voice; I know them,
and they follow me. John 10:27 NIV

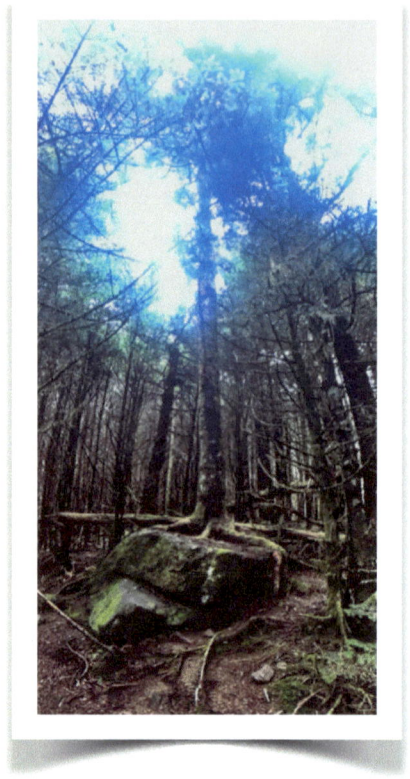

Direct me in the path of your commands,
for there I find delight. Psalm 119:35 NIV

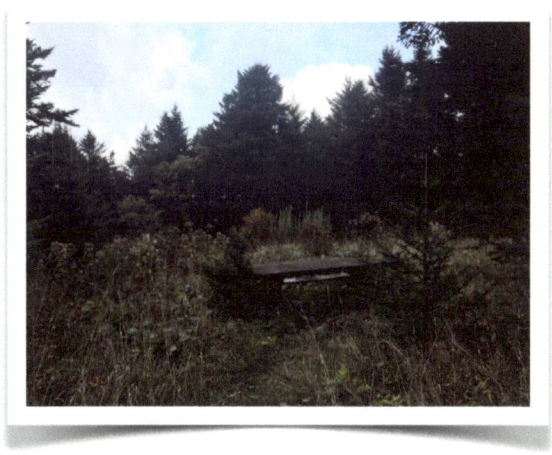

Jesus answered, "I am the way and the truth and the life. No one comes to the Father except through me. John 14:6 NIV

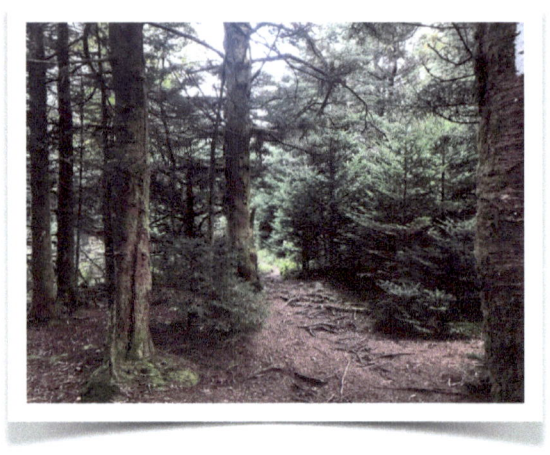

Though he may stumble, he will not fall,
for the Lord upholds him with his hand.
Psalm 37:24 NIV

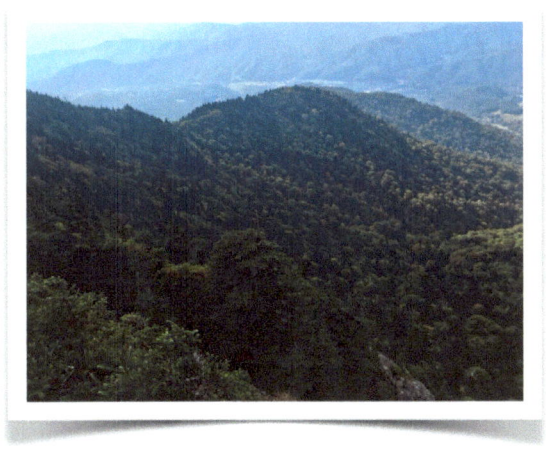

For your ways are in full view of the Lord,
and he examines all your paths.
Proverbs 5:21 NIV

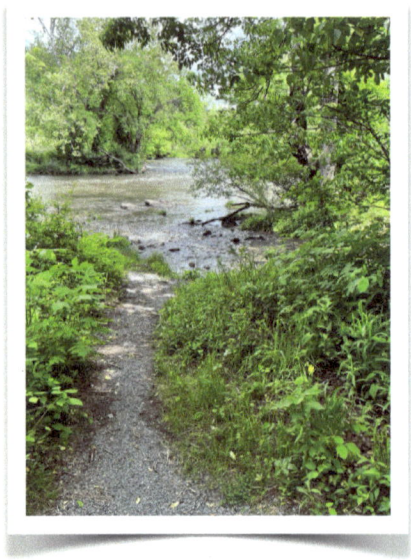

When you pass through the waters, I will be with you; and when you pass through the rivers, they will not sweep over you. When you walk through the fire, you will not be burned; the flames will not set you ablaze. Isaiah 43:2 NIV

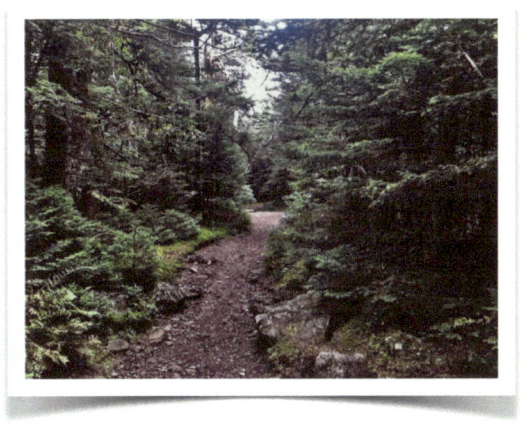

I keep my eyes always on the Lord. With him
at my right hand, I will not be shaken.
Psalm 16:8 NIV

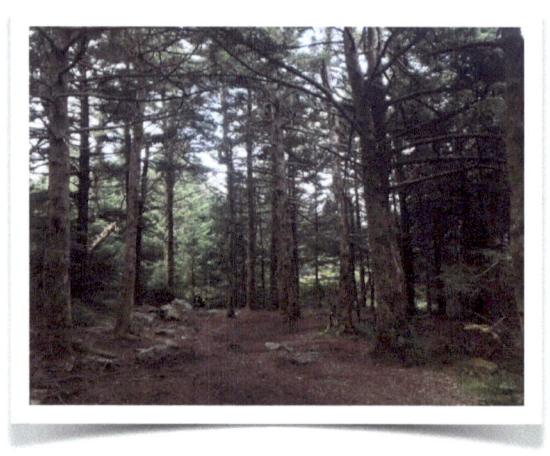

Show me your ways, Lord, teach me your paths. Guide me in your truth and teach me, for you are God my Savior, and my hope is in you all day long. Psalm 25:4-5 NIV

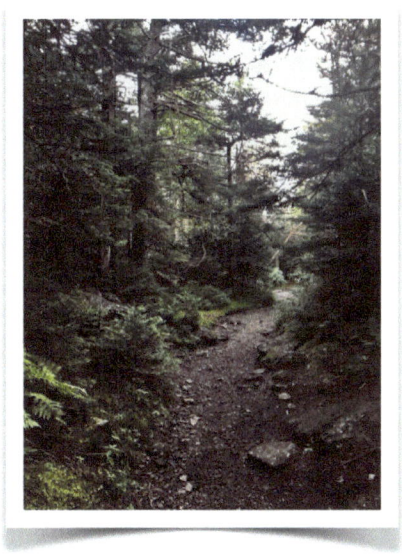

Since you are my rock and my fortress, for
the sake of your name lead and guide me.
Psalm 31:3 NIV

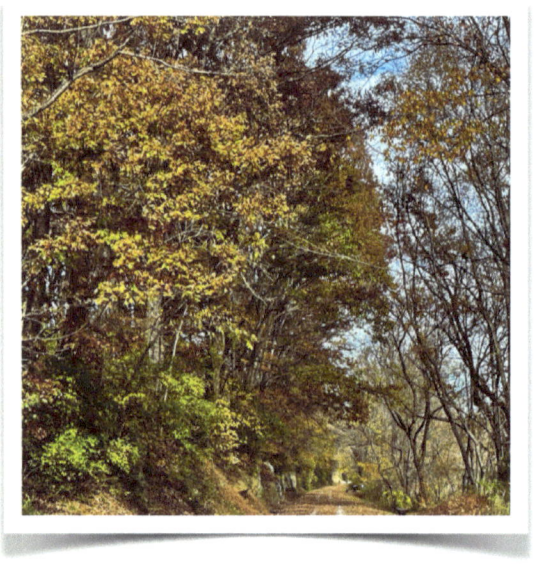

Do not be wise in your own eyes; fear the
Lord and shun evil. Proverbs 3:7 NIV

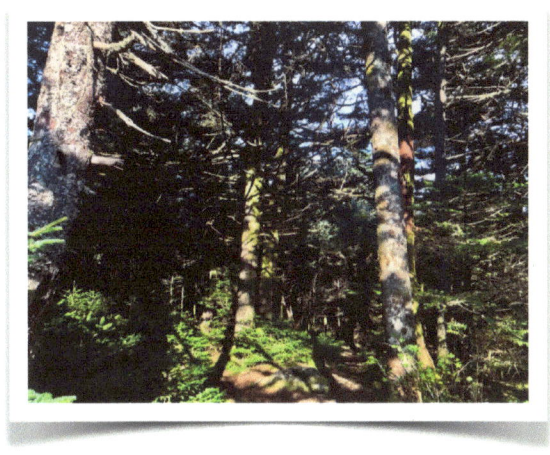

You discern my going out and my lying down;
you are familiar with all my ways.
Psalm 139:3 NIV

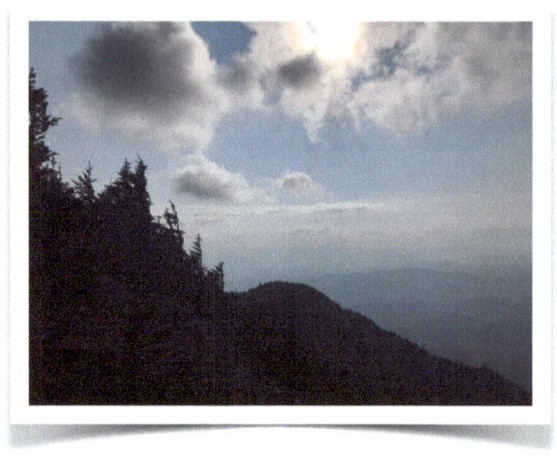

A person may think their own ways are right,
but the Lord weighs the heart.
Proverbs 21:2 NIV

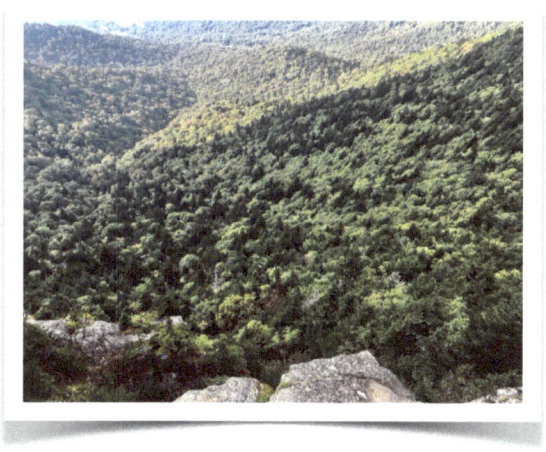

Commit to the Lord whatever you do,
and he will establish your plans.
Proverbs 16:3 NIV

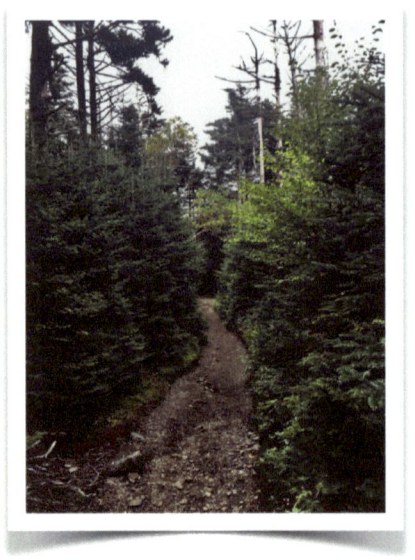

For I know the plans I have for you," declares the
Lord, "plans to prosper you and not to harm you,
plans to give you hope and a future.
Jeremiah 29:11 NIV

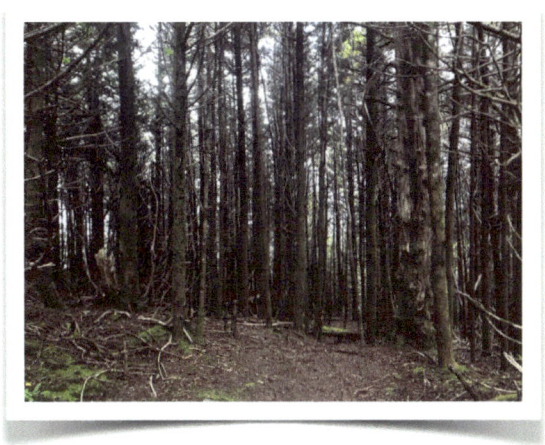

Blessed are those who find wisdom, those
who gain understanding, Proverbs 3:13 NIV

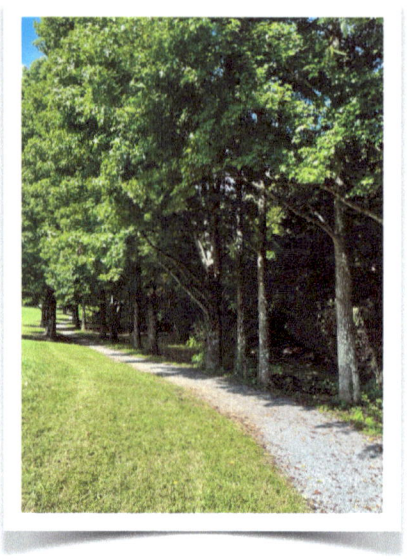

but whoever listens to me will live in safety and be at ease, without fear of harm. Proverbs 1:33 NIV

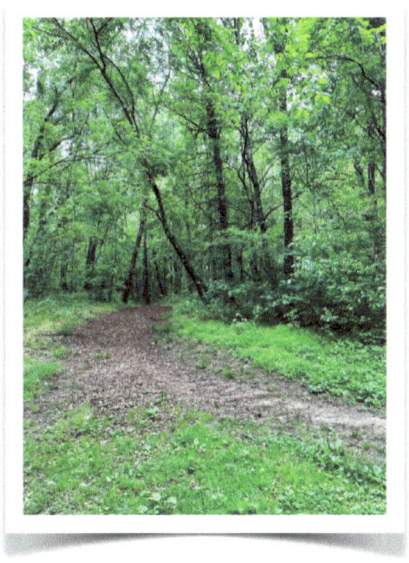

Commit your way to the Lord; trust in
him and he will do this Psalm 37:5 NIV

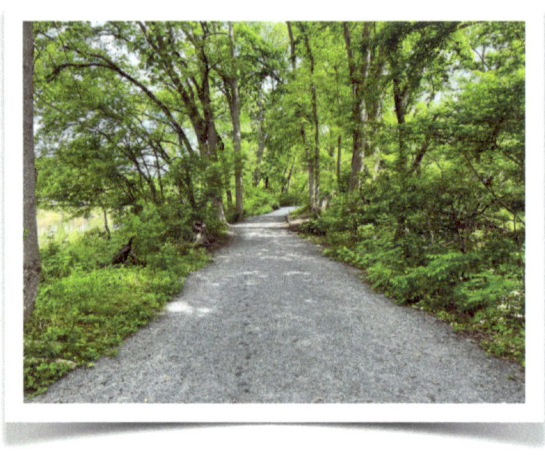

I will lead the blind by ways they have not known,
along unfamiliar paths I will guide them; I will
turn the darkness into light before them and make
the rough places smooth.These are the things I will
do; I will not forsake them. Isaiah 42:16 NIV

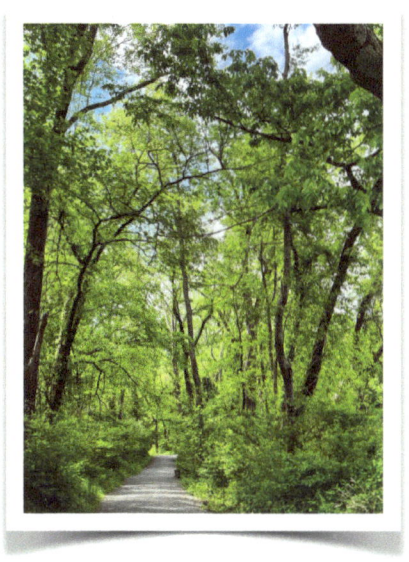

I instruct you in the way of wisdom
and lead you along straight paths.
Proverbs 4:11 NIV

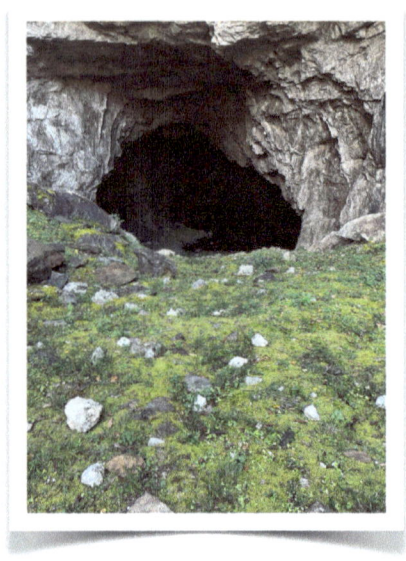

Since you are my rock and my fortress,
for the sake of your name lead and
guide me. Psalms 31:3 NIV

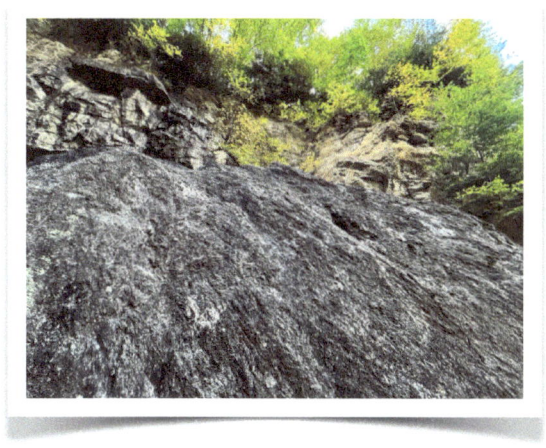

When I am afraid, I put my trust in you.
Psalms 56:3 NIV

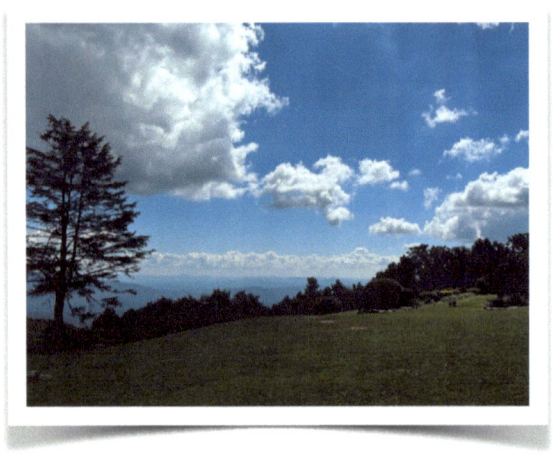

May the God of hope fill you with all joy and peace as you trust in him, so that you may overflow with hope by the power of the Holy Spirit. Romans 15:13 NIV

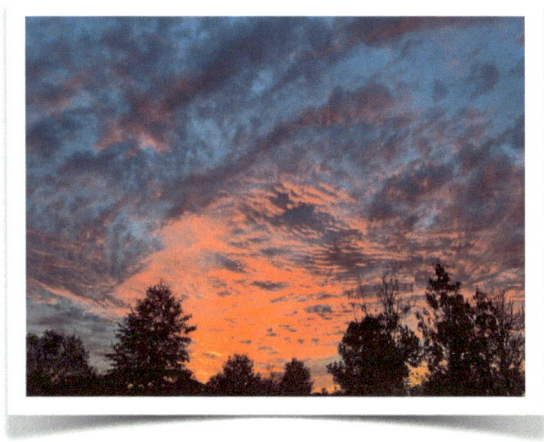

And we know that in all things God works for the good of those who love him, who have been called according to his purpose. Romans 8:28 NIV

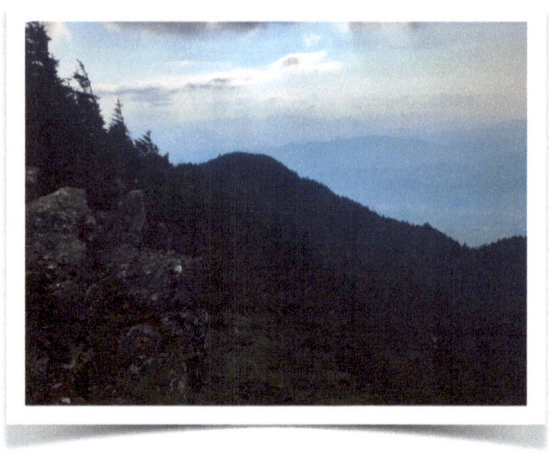

Find Joy In The Journey

We can leave behind the past and embark on new
journeys as the path leads us from the mountain
tops through the valleys. The path we take,
whether right or wrong, awaits. Let God guide
you on the correct path, and remember to
enjoy the journey.

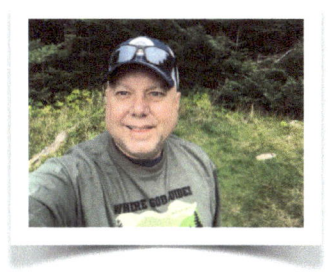

About the Author GW Tolley

GW Tolley is an International Author, Self-Publishing Coach, Udemy Instructor (SELF PUBLISHING-Outside the Box), Amazon Best Sellers Rank, Writer / Executive Producer of "i am JOSIAH" Project, TV Host / Executive Producer of "What's Your Story," Co-Host of Lessons For Life/Abundant TV, Google Influencer (77+ Million views), Podcaster, YouTuber, Awareness Advocate (Homeless, Underprivileged, Hearing Impaired and Deaf), WRITE It OUT Program (Firefighters, First Responders, Military, and Police Officers), all this is God's doing.

GW Tolley's Story

Let's dig a little deeper into who GW is.

What do hearing loss, purpose, "Don't be a Jonah," and a lost sheep all have in common? Let's see. Read on.

A recent situation involving my hearing was an unnerving reminder of how precious our hearing is —and brought back a flood of emotions. I am fine, but the scars are always there. A word of advice: Wear your scars with pride. I do. We cannot have a testimony without a test.

I had ear issues from birth, and that went on until my second year of high school. I was constantly at the doctor's, and the medicine he prescribed tasted nasty. When the medicine ran out, the issues would come right back—sometimes worse than before. When I was younger, they removed my tonsils to see if this would correct the issue, but it did not. Not only did I have a hard time hearing, but my last name began with a T, and my seat was in the back of the room at school. Unable to hear, I would get bored and doodle, and my mind would wander everywhere. A grade of C- or even a D+ was a significant accomplishment. My mom would work with me with flash cards. She would say, "You are smart and can do anything you put your mind to.

There is always a way around, over, or under every situation, and sometimes you must go through it." My momma was kind, intelligent, and business savvy, but if you messed with her family or children, that is another story.

One day, my mom noticed I had the TV turned up loud. It was total volume; there was not another notch to turn it higher. She returned me to the doctor and told him, "Send him to a specialist. He cannot hear." I was referred to an ear, nose, and throat specialist and found out I had 95% hearing loss in one of my ears. I had surgery right then and there because of the severity of my situation (tubes inserted to correct the issue). They brought in a machine that was like a giant vacuum cleaner. There was a big needle. The doctor said, "I am going to bust your eardrum, and you will hear a strange noise. We will vacuum out the liquid." The liquid was almost black. The noise was thunderous and nearly unbearable. They could not numb my ear, and I just had to be a big boy and tough it out. My mom said, "Be strong. I am right here with you." I did well, and she wiped the only tear from my eye.

Keep moving forward and be an overcomer. My mom would say, "Keep your feet on the ground, but reach for the stars." So, with all that being said, if anyone had told me I would write a book, much less 21 plus books, I would have laughed at them and said, "No, not me! You are mistaken. You have the wrong guy." English, spelling, grammar, punctuation—that is not me.

"Thank You, God, and thank you for the editors," I tell it like it is, and sometimes it's just the raw truth. Occasionally, that is hard for people to handle, but it is what it is.

When you have a story, and it feels like you will explode if you don't tell it, whether you like it or not, you have to get it out of your system. Release it and get it out. That is what happened to me. The stories had to come out—the pain, the hurt, the shame, the tears of sorrow, and joy. Write even when it is uncomfortable because one of the best ways to heal is to get it out. People are going to talk about you no matter what you do. You cannot control what they say or what happens, but you can control how you respond or don't respond. When you do that, you are in control of yourself—and that is powerful. NEVER let people, where you came from, or your circumstances dictate who you are and where you are going! You have a purpose; I have a purpose; we all have a Kingdom purpose.

Jeremiah 29:11, "For I know the plans I have for you," declares the Lord, "plans to prosper you and not to harm you, plans to give you hope and a future."

As a child, I was dragged to church Sunday morning, night, and Wednesday every time the doors opened. I vowed when I was older that I would never go to church again. I did not go for 20 years. I was a very angry, drunk, and mean prodigal son. You would never have heard me speak of God (God of Abraham, Isaac, and Jacob). I believed He was there, but I would not discuss Him.

Excessively partying with fair-weather friends, I went down many wrong roads. The storms of my life had begun, and I did not know until it was too late. The unstoppable chain of events started with identity theft in June 2009 and led to my home being foreclosed on Christmas Eve and later padlocked. 98% of my possessions were donated to charity. I was homeless and then laid off. Out of desperation, I placed an ad on Craigslist for a place to live. I ended up living with a family of nine.

Some nights, I had no food. I would microwave water to fill my stomach so that it had something warm so I could go to sleep. I ate oatmeal for two years, and finally, I dropped my pride and went to a food bank. Ironically, I volunteered at that food bank, but I was too prideful and ashamed to go through the program. They quickly said, "Raise your head!" They shared that they had started as a client and now volunteered. "No shame here," they said. The most overwhelming challenge was losing my mom. Over a span of years, she died four times, and on two occasions, she was gone for over thirty minutes—but came back to life! There is power in prayer, and miracles happen every day. Finally, however, the day came when she died and graduated to Heaven. It was her time. (The Bible tells us in Psalm 139:16, "…all the days ordained for me were written in your book before one of them came to be.")

A significant turning point was when I fell asleep while driving, and my car headed toward a transformer pole. A man called and woke me up. He said, "God told me that you were in danger and to call you. Your divine life purpose is much needed in the world. I have to stay on the phone with you until you're parked."

I know God saved my life that day.
I had to change my" Whys" into "I trust You." I had to stop whining and being a Jeremiah. I had to stop saying, "Please take away these burdens." Instead, I had to pray for faith, broader shoulders, strength, and seeing others as God's children and not judging them. I also had to learn to forgive. Giving situations to God, I started watching my words. A few words of kindness can change a

person's day or life. This process was about learning to be Christ-like, selfless, unshakeable faith, hope, and love. It involved listening to God and being obedient.

God has given me the strength and the courage to take one step at a time. Throughout this 10-year process, He has made a way—in His time and in a unique way. I share my stories because my trials have become my testimonies. My life has been restored and blessed. God has made His masterpiece out of my mess. To God be ALL the praise and glory! I want people to see Him, not me.

God has revealed my Kingdom PURPOSE. I would never have guessed it in a million years—or even thought about sharing or speaking about His FORGIVENESS and GRACE. But here I am. I have stopped fighting my calling.

Don't be a Jonah (Jonah 1-4), and don't do what I did—run for 20-plus years, then be in a 10-year learning process. "Just don't!" is all I can say—it is painful. Embrace God's LOVE and His MERCY.

People have said, "We see that GW found Jesus." However, the truth is that Jesus found me! Every day, I thank Him for pursuing me. I was that one lost sheep.

Questions and Answers = Resources

1.) QUESTION
Who is God

ANSWER
God from the Holy Bible: The God of Abraham, Isaac, and Jacob. Jesus Christ LORD and SAVIOR.

2.) QUESTION
Let me ask you a question, a very important question. If you should die today, are you 100% certain that you are going to Heaven?

If you should die today and stand before God, and He asked you why He should let you into His Heaven, what would you say?

ANSWER
Did you know that you can be 100% certain you are going to Heaven? You CAN know, and here is how. In 1 John 5:13, the Bible says, "I write these things to you who believe in the name of the Son of God so that you may know that you have eternal life."

In Romans 3:10 the Bible says, "As it is written: There is no one righteous, not even one." and in verse 23, "For all have sinned and fall short of the glory of God." That means I'm a sinner, and that means you are a sinner also. Most people do not realize the seriousness of sin. God is holy, and sin separates a sinner from God.

This verse shows how serious it is! In Romans 5:12 the Bible says, "Therefore, just as sin entered the world through one man, and death through sin, and in this way death came to all people, because all have sinned." The word "death" doesn't mean dying and going to the grave; it means separation from God. Until our sins are forgiven, we are separated from God on this earth, and we will be separated from God forever and ever in a place called Hell. This is the punishment for our sin. But the story doesn't end here! In Romans 6:23 the Bible says, "For the wages of sin is death, but the gift of God is eternal life in Christ Jesus our Lord." The words "eternal life" mean more than living forever; they mean to live forever in Heaven. Notice that being saved is a gift—it's absolutely free! You can't buy it, work for it, or be good enough for it. It is free! It would be as if a friend went to the store and purchased you a present. They paid for it, wrapped it, put a bow on it, and brought it to you. They did everything for you. All you have to do is receive it.

That is what Jesus did! He left His home in Heaven, came to earth, died on the cross, shed His blood, and paid for your sins. He did everything for you. All you have to do is receive it. Romans 5:8 says He did this for us while we were still sinners.

Most people think they have to stop doing everything bad before God will save them. But God loves us as sinners, and Jesus died for us. When Jesus died for you, He made it possible for you to have forgiveness of sins and eternal life with God. However, just because Jesus died for you, that does not automatically save you. The following is Yes or No answers. You must ask Jesus to forgive your sins.

1.) Now, do you admit that you are a sinner?

2.) Do you understand that sin separates you from God?

3.) Do you believe Jesus died on the cross for you?

4.) Would you like to be forgiven of all your sins and know 100% you are going to Heaven?

If YES, then this is what you need to do.
In Romans 10:9-13 the Bible tells us that if you call upon the name of the Lord, you will be saved. Then, according to the Bible, if you asked Jesus into your heart right now, He will save you forever! Wouldn't you like to do this? If you will

trust Jesus to take you to Heaven when you die, pray this prayer.

"Dear Jesus, I know I am a sinner. I believe You died for my sins and God raised You from the dead. Forgive me of all my sins. Come into my heart today. Give me a home in Heaven when I die. Help me to obey You. I mean this prayer with all my heart!"

Romans 10:13 says, "For everyone who calls on the name of the Lord will be saved."

If you have done this, then according to the Bible, you are saved—and if you were to die today, you would go to Heaven!

I also encourage you to: 1) Read the Bible so that you can grow in your faith—maybe start with the first four books of the New Testament: Matthew, Mark, Luke, and John. To help you to learn more about the Bible, I suggest you also go to www.BibleHub.com. 2) Pray to God—He cares for you. Jesus gives an example of how to pray in Matthew 6:9-13. 3) Find a Bible-based church— one that not only teaches the Bible but will help you to grow in your faith. 4) Be baptized (Matthew 28:19-20)

After this manner therefore pray ye: Our Father which art in heaven, Hallowed be thy name. Thy

kingdom come, Thy will be done in earth, as it is in heaven. Give us this day our daily bread. And forgive us our debts, as we forgive our debtors. And lead us not into temptation, but deliver us from evil: For thine is the kingdom, and the power, and the glory, for ever. Amen.
Matthew 6:9-13 (KJV)

3.) QUESTION
The Lord is my Shepard

ANSWER
The Lord is my shepherd, I lack nothing. He makes me lie down in green pastures, he leads me beside quiet waters, he refreshes my soul. He guides me along the right paths for his name's sake. Even though I walk through the darkest valley, I will fear no evil, for you are with me; your rod and your staff, they comfort me. You prepare a table before me in the presence of my enemies. You anoint my head with oil; my cup overflows. Surely your goodness and love will follow me all the days of my life, and I will dwell in the house of the Lord forever. Psalm 23

4.) QUESTION
WHEN YOU HEAR THAT VOICE Sounds Good ~ Not Sure ? Ask !!! Test it!!!

ANSWER

Do you confess that Jesus is the Messiah who came in the flesh from God? "By this you know the Spirit of God: every spirit that confesses that Jesus Christ has come in the flesh is from God; and every spirit that does not confess Jesus is not from God; this is the spirit of the antichrist, of which you have heard that it is coming, and now it is already in the world."1 John 4:2-3

5.) QUESTION

How to Bold and Cast Out Unholy, Unclean Spirits that are not of God.

ANSWER

Unholy, Unclean Spirits Bind and Cast-Out in Jesus name Amen.

Do You Have Stories?

What is STOPPING YOU from Self-Publishing?

You have a book idea, and now what?
How to start your book process, starting from the foundation and building upwards, one step at a time. Whether you are writing a fiction/non-fiction book, children's book, cookbook, or biography, this book breaks down the process and explains all the how-to's from start to finish.

The main goal is to get your book out into the world. How to get started, book size, margins, book covers and different styles, types of self-publishing, Amazon/Kindle, ISBN, barcodes, copyright, domain, book category, self-fulfillment, co-authors, and special guest, brand, corporate seal, audiobooks, audio booth 101, one thing could lead to another, tv, radio, podcast, newspaper or a movie.

Did you know? Selecting a book size that is not "STANDARD" could lead to your book not being printed in some countries. No one wants lost sales. So, being Unique or Creative might hinder your book sales and your story going worldwide. The

World is Waiting for your story. Get started today; you can do this.

Empower Your Dreams: Turn Your Book Idea into a Reality Today!

What is STOPPING YOU from Self-Publishing by GW Tolley is available on Amazon Paperback and KDP ebook.

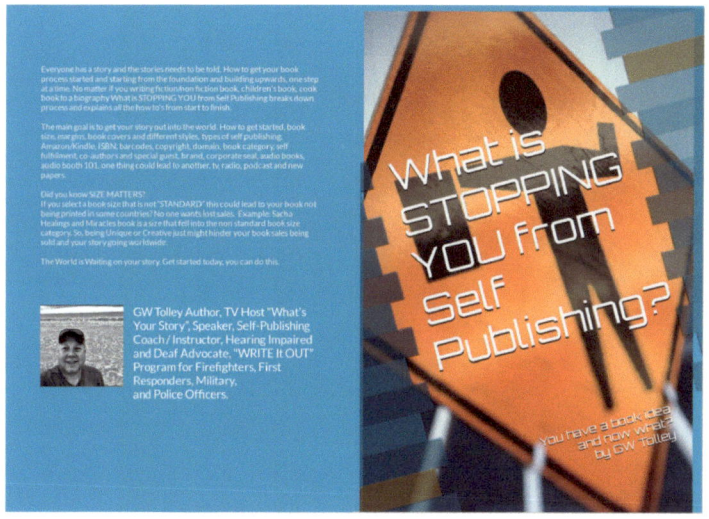

"i am JOSIAH" Project
www.iamJosiahProject.com

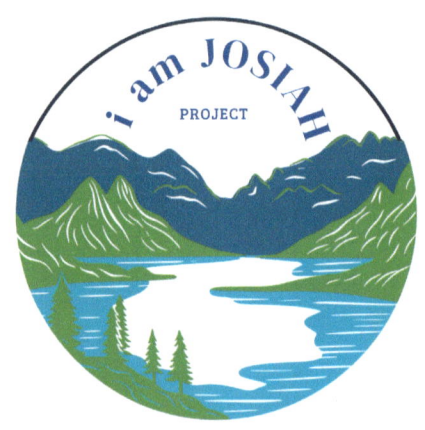

The Bridge of Faith by TK Hinkle is about actual events. What begins as a typical workday takes an unexpected turn, bringing multiple people with various occupations and diverse places together for one goal. Many of these people's minds and lives will never be the same. It's a testimony of faith, hope, and courage in adversity.

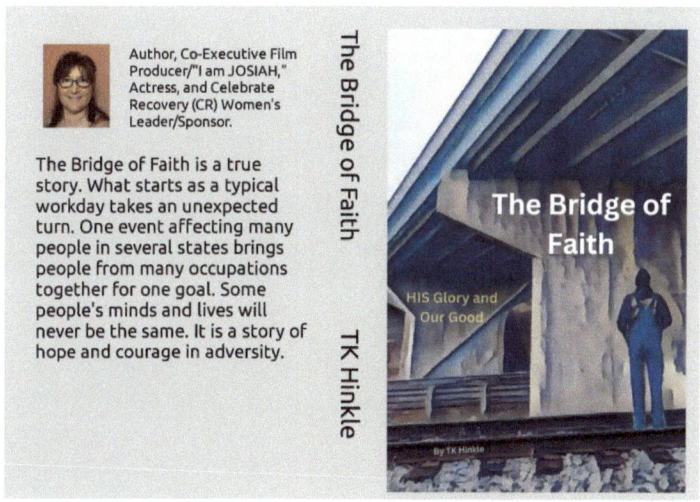

The Bridge of Faith by TK Hinkle is available on Amazon (paperback) and Kindle (ebook).

THANK YOU

BLESSING

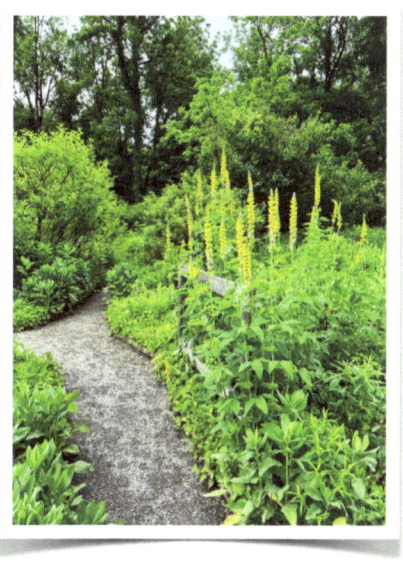

The LORD bless you and keep you; The LORD make His face shine upon you, And be gracious to you; The LORD lift up His countenance upon you, And give you peace. Numbers 6:24–26 NIV

www.ingramcontent.com/pod-product-compliance
Lightning Source LLC
Chambersburg PA
CBHW042038230526
45474CB00005B/14